Katharyn Howd Machan

SELECTED POEMS

FUTURECYCLE PRESS
www.futurecycle.org

Cover image, "D. auratus sub-adults" by Erik Mattheis; cover and interior book design by Diane Kistner; Gentium Book Basic text and Cronos Pro titling

Library of Congress Control Number: 2017961610

Published by FutureCycle Press
Athens, Georgia, USA

ISBN 978-1-942371-44-1

for Eric, Beloved since 1990

Contents

From
WILD GRAPES: POEMS OF FOX

From
DARK MATTERS

Foreword

Katharyn Howd Machan: Selected Poems traces the literary journey of a woman who has been following the writing path, no matter how dark the woods, since the age of fifteen. Machan grew up in Woodbury, Connecticut, and Pleasantville, New York. She studied creative writing and literature at the College of Saint Rose (BA) and the University of Iowa (MA), and Interpretation (Performance Studies) at Northwestern University (PhD). Now a full professor in the Department of Writing, Machan has been teaching on the faculty of Ithaca College for forty years, with additional roles in Women's Studies, the Gerontology Institute, and the First-Year Seminar Program. Her poems have appeared in numerous journals such as *Nimrod, Yankee, The MacGuffin Reader, Snake Nation Review, Hanging Loose, Dogwood, Runes, Slipstream, The Beloit Poetry Journal, South Coast Poetry Journal, The Hollins Critic, The Salmon, West Branch, Seneca Review,* and *Louisiana Literature* and in anthologies and textbooks such as *The Bedford Introduction to Literature, The Best American Nonrequired Reading, Poetry: An Introduction, Early Ripening: American Women's Poetry Now, Sound and Sense, Writing Poems,* and *Literature: Reading and Writing the Human Experience.* She has published thirty-four previous collections of poetry (an amazing achievement) and was awarded the Ann Stanford Poetry Prize from the University of Southern California by judge Dana Gioia for her poem "Tess Clarion: Redwing, 1888." She also won the Luna Negra Prize from Kent State University for her poem "Gingerbread" and was named the first Poet Laureate of Tompkins County, New York, in 2002.

As Zajal, Machan is also a professional belly dancer, celebrating spirituality and laughter, with a special interest in combining dance and poetry in performances and workshops, as reflected in her chapbook *Belly Words.* In this capacity, she taught for many years at the Community School of Music and Arts in Ithaca, New York, and on the Aegean island of Skyros for the United Kingdom-based Skyros Institute, which emphasizes holistic studies. She also offers, in her persona as the Sugarplum Fairy, original audience-participation StoryDance performances for and with children.

In this selected poems volume, Machan takes us on an extended voyage through her many volumes of poetry, including raccoons as myth-making tricksters, feminist takes on fairy tales, classical mythology, the personal mythology of her family (her mother, the good time girl; her troubled brother, the abuser), her travels to France (where "the sun fills air / with bay and lavender") and Greece ("bold blue breezeswept sky of hot gold sun"), her loves and lovers, her children (one son and one daughter, "a fierceness where my heart // once beat alone"), her commitment to dance ("My ankles offer golden bells that sing of light and wonder"), and her appreciation of food ("The Beets Poem," "Potatoes").

With the fractured fairy tale, "Hazel Tells LaVerne," her most widely reprinted poem (written in the voice of one motel cleaning maid speaking to another), Machan gives us a unique reworking of the tale of the princess and the frog. Sometimes writing in form, she is a master (mistress) of the sonnet. One collection of sonnets chronicles the life of the Professor, a decidedly male academic poet. Another collection, using free verse, tells of Fox, a female shapeshifter able to be fully human, fully beast, or a combination of the two. In a full-length collection begun in 1985 and published in 2005, Machan shapes dramatic monologues with different personae and voices to tell the stories of women, men, and children living in the imagined town of Redwing, New York, in 1888. There are also dark poems, especially those in the chapbook *H*, that respond to her daughter's heroin addiction and the terror of being a mother unable to save her child.

Machan honors Wise Woman, the Crone, the Goddess, in poem after poem. She looks Death in the eye and welcomes her in with this gorgeous personification: "When Death comes riding on her crimson broom, / heed her. Sing praises to her copper eye / that counts silk threads before they reach the loom / and spiders them to patterns a dark sky / calls friend."

About some of the individual collections

Just like Edgar Lee Masters in *Spoon River Anthology*, Machan's *Redwing: Voices from 1888* creates a fictional town, this one in rural central/western New York, and makes it come alive through a series of linked monologues. Even though these poems are cast in the late nineteenth century, they are as timely as the daily newspaper concerning the things that matter most— weddings, births, deaths. These stories burn to be told, and this is the writer who was born to tell them.

Sleeping with the Dead is a haunting collection of poems of mourning and loss, ranging from the public and national grief over September 11, 2001, to the personal and private, the suicide of her brother. These poems will break your heart, then mend it again; they will take you on a journey into darkness, to places as exotic and far away as Key West and Prague, and leave you dancing in light.

Wise Woman has the best batch of titles on the block: "Wise Woman Lets Her Glasses Slide Where Keys and Screen Say Yes," "Wise Woman Counts the Times She's Laughed and Packs Them in a Basket," "Wise Woman's Friend Paints Her Portrait on a Canvas Stretched Beyond Time," and my all-time favorite, "Wise Woman Turns Her Tenure File into a Forest of Birds." Machan's decades of belly dancing have helped to shape the sense of rhythm throughout this book, sure and insistent as a doumbek, the drum central to Middle Eastern music. In the late 1990s Jean Burden, poetry editor of *Yankee*, wrote,

"Her work is characterized by exact observation, fresh images that tingle and surprise, and a point of view that is never expected." Listen to this stanza from "Wise Woman Weaves a Magic Carpet to Travel Where Light Shapes":

> soon she'll rub Aladdin's lamp
> soon she'll nest the phoenix egg
> soon she'll stitch a magic bag
> that opens when she smiles

Between these pages, we meet Wise Woman in her many guises: Eve ("Wise Woman Ventures into Eden but Prefers a Good Hot Meal"), Scheherazade (the abovementioned "Weaves a Magic Carpet"), the Crone ("Wise Woman Goes a Little Crazy a Decade or Two Here and There"), and Death ("Wise Woman Talks About Her Sister, the One Most People Shun"), to mention some. Look at all the precise images in "Wise Woman Goes a Little Crazy":

> she affects eccentricity:
> poodle hat, pink corduroy,
> a loop of broken rosary beads
> dangling at her throat

There is some terrific music created when "affects" and "eccentricity" rub up against each other, creating sparks. These sparks ignite their own kind of fire, candles dancing in the darkness, lighting the way. Maybe cowgirls get the blues, but Wise Woman doesn't; she's brassy and sassy as the sun on a long summer day. As Machan celebrates her, we begin to realize that Wise Woman is all of us; in fact, she could be me.

Skyros, a collection of twenty sonnets written during one of Machan's sojourns teaching dance and poetry on that Aegean isle, transports us oceans away to a small island in sun-soaked Greece, where "the bay curves emerald, turquoise," and you walk on ancient cobbled streets to a village "clustered up a hill," "walls of weathered white," "sheltered...for shade against the long sun." Listen to the call of drums and bells. Smell basil in pots by every door. Machan beckons us to "turn and dance within the light," and we do, we do.

What else are poems, but love letters to the universe? What else is the work of Katharyn Howd Machan but a love letter to us all?

—Barbara Crooker

author of *Les Fauves* (C&R Press) and
Barbara Crooker: Selected Poems (FutureCycle Press)

From

THE RACCOON BOOK

(McBooks Press, 1982)

When They Lined Up for the Ark

the raccoons waited.
They believed in unicorns
surviving
but the great white patriarch
said no they are too whimsical
irreverent and downright
obscene with those shining golden horns
sticking it up heaven.
So the raccoons held back
but the sons caught them offguard
and slapped hands over their eyes,
dragging them into the wooden boat
against their will, saving them.
That's why raccoons wear masks,
in memory of unicorns.

Sometimes

when a raccoon is treed
she jumps down hard
breaking
the mad dog's back.

Her Great Great Grandmother

came to her in a dream,
teeth bared in an affectionate grin.
"Child," she said, "you should know
I was born part raccoon.
That's why I survived
all the days of empty doors,
all the nights with no sound but my own.
And that's why you'll survive 'em, too."

Upon waking she arose
to wash her thoughts in water.
As she glanced into the bathroom mirror
she saw for the first time
the outline of a mask around her eyes.

From
WRITING HOME
(with Barbara Crooker)

(Gehry Press, 1983)

Cinderella's Mice

We knew it was the end:
black metal bars, no crumbs remaining,
only our dark eyes shining
at the thin fur of each other's throats.
The cook would drown us in an iron pail,
set the trap anew, think nothing
of the hunger that had led us to this place.
We knew. It was our fate.

But then the black bars turned to air.
Freed, we stared in disbelief, then ran
for well-known tunnels, hearts pounding glad
as paws scrabbled across cold stone.
We never made it. Those paws grew
to hooves, our gray tails plumed,
we wore bells and ribbons on proud heads
that tossed in full-maned splendor.
The kitchen shrank away. We pranced
in harness, a golden coach behind
and all the velvet night before us
spangled with a thousand dreams.
The royal road gleamed strange and new.
We neighed, alive with more than life,
and learned to stamp, to trot, to pull
the silver girl in small glass shoes
towards a destiny she could not meet
without us. How we moved!

Then the clock struck twelve.
The reins sank back, limp vines,
the music ceased, the velvet hung in strings;
we blinked in chilling darkness once again.
Coach gone, girl gone, gold and silver
a mound of rotting fruit and rags.

Where do we turn? What destiny?
Uncaged, we are supposed to run away,
but tunnels hold no comfort for us now

and food no longer pulls us from our dreams.
We huddle here where once we pranced,
bereft, bewildered—free to wonder only
at the new hunger that gnaws our hearts
and will not let us be.

Five Poets Travel to and from a Poetry Reading Two Hours Away

He is a mechanic.
It is his car; he drives it;
it is his birthday.
Every day he thinks about the Orient.
Once he wrote a poem
about deer with diamond eyes.

She is a stranger,
except to the mechanic
who holds her hand, her shoulders.
She is his birthday present,
a poem in flesh.

She is an actress/dancer
who has lived in Mexico
and who has dated Margaret Mead's stepson,
a handsome blond jock with brains, and who
makes three dollars an hour
modeling naked, and who tells about it.
Her eyes are large and green
and her face is an opening flower.

He is a microbiologist.
He wears loose glasses,
a handsome beard; he
fidgets with it. His talk is
brilliant, diffuse,
sometimes inarticulate.
He has a willing heart
and sometimes he writes poetry.

She is an English teacher.
She loves the microbiologist;
she is married to him.
She leans against a door,
writing this poem in her head
in the back seat
while the microbiologist

talks and talks to the actress/dancer
about things her green eyes have observed.

It is raining
and the deer running from the roadside
does have diamond eyes
and the woman in the front
is still a stranger
and the husband leans close
against the silent wife,
compensating
for the widening green eyes.

Black Swans: A Poem for Voices

for the Feminist Women's Writing Workshops, Inc.

We are the black swans,
the women who swim.
Who fly at night.
Who are the night.
Our golden feet touch
quiet water, skim
shining surface, plunge deep
to make currents in dark weeds.
We come and go.
We know each other's
names, each other's dreams;
we dream each other.
Dream the flight
past ragged moon,
past singing stars,
and it comes true.
Dream the telling,
the shapes of rain
and frogs and light,
and it comes true.
We are the wings.
We reach for wind
and make it ours;
we become the wind.
Our words are swan words,
black and full.
We go distances,
return, endure.

From

WHEN SHE WAS THE GOOD-TIME GIRL

(The Signpost Press, 1987)

When She Was the Good-time Girl, My Mother

(circa 1931)

When she was the good-time girl, my mother
wore black velvet, pleased the men, danced
the fox trot slow and easy all night long.
She kept her hair cut short and tight
and plucked her eyebrows high and thin
and danced danced the samba, stars to dawn.

When she was the good-time girl, my mother
knew the moves and found the doctor
who would keep her secrets, keep her clean.
She wore red lipstick, smoked cigarettes,
laughed and laughed through beaded hours
and dabbed her careful neckline with My Sin.

When she was the good-time girl, my mother
ate and drank what men would buy her,
kissed them hard, took what they gave.
Then she saw that time was moving
and married one who loved her face
and whispered to her mirror, "Now I'm saved."

In 1929

My mother got laid at seventeen
and didn't know what had happened.
It was an older man (at least twenty-two)
and he split the next day
for the Indianapolis Speedway.
When my mother got home that night
she threw her underclothes into the bathroom
and my grandmother found them
and examined them, with that gleam
in her eye I remember oh so well.
"What did you do?" she demanded, knowing.
My mother said, "Nothing," and my grandmother
slapped her and said, "You're ruined."
So my mother went on to take
twelve lovers before she married at twenty-one.
She knew what *ruined* meant
then, and knew it counted.

Journey through the Door
into Always-Always Land: 1966

Between my father's death
and my first kiss
it came,
the blood suddenly there
maroon on my cotton underpants
in that chill Long Island
Howard Johnson's ladies' room.
That was the first time
I bit the wings off fried butterfly
shrimp, too;
I have always suspected a correlation.

We'd gone to visit my brother's godfather
with the giant hobby train set
racing through his cellar.
When we got back from lunch
with the brown-bagged box
discreetly tucked under my mother's arm
his wife showed us upstairs
and my mother closed the bathroom door
proud with the Mystery
and said   *You know from the books*
I gave you what is happening.
Did I ever tell you (she had told me)
how when I was 11 (I was 13)
I fell from a tree (I had eaten the shrimp)
and later the bleeding began and I thought
I was hurt but your grandmother said
suspiciously sniffing my underclothes
No   It's something all women get
The Curse   Accept it
You'll be all right   You'll have to put up
with it from now on   Here use these rags   *and*
she showed me how to pin them on
and later how to wash them out
over and over and over.
At least things are more comfortable now.
I listened to the words suddenly real

watching her take out the tiny mattress and
show me how to hook it on
the pink elastic belly belt.
We went down the flights of stairs
(my thighs burning aware and clumsy)
into the godfather's wife's welcoming smile
down to the big room
full of the stench of electricity
where the long sleek train
rushed round and around so powerful.
Where've you been? my big brother crowed.
Tell us where, oh where you have been.

In This Hotel Called Home

Christmas Day and you were drunk again,
handing out presents like a maitre d'.
The tinsel tree lights flashed behind you,
red and yellow, blue and green. We tore
ribbons and silver paper to find
things in boxes no one needs,
cheap clothes and gadgets from catalogues
that cost you two weeks' pay.
How proud you were of vinyl gloves,
plastic bookends bumpy with glue,
even a nutcracker from Taiwan
that broke at our first squeeze.

Christmas with cookies and chocolate again,
your fat bottle of whiskey sporting
a crimson Santa coat and cap.
We gave you nightgowns and cologne,
three pairs of slippers, a lacy apron,
even seven cartons of cigarettes
that screamed *Mother!* in their wrapping.
Fruit, turkey, plum pudding aflame:
you smiled and giggled through it all
as Santa's buttons and belt came askew.

At last, by the fire, you fell asleep,
your head dropped back for a tippler's snore.
Then we turned to each other, uneasy,
judging who'd be the first to go
and who'd linger to wake you for bed.
Again we hid the truth of this Christmas,
Christmases past and to come:
in this room strewn with disappointments
it is only you who offers love.

My Brother

My brother lives in a box of cigars.
Each day every day
he lifts the lid to peek at the world
and hopes the world won't notice.
Bristles grow on his face and throat.
He smells, fears soap.
He never throws his loose hairs away
but carefully keeps them, dirty and dark,
in the teeth of a green plastic comb.

Long ago he spent years committing incest.
I survived but we never mention it.
He's thirty-five now and still lives with our mother.
My favorite joke when I visit is to talk
of the time I stabbed his thigh with a fork
and sent him screeching around the table
for ruining my first perfect crayoned picture.
We pretend to laugh and the scar
does not go away. Migraine headaches
take me back to the fork, to the fort
he built under cool pines
where he wouldn't let me visit
unless I would...and I did.

Now he does his best to repel.
He rots his teeth, sucks his cigars,
growls and belches and grows fat.
Each night every night
he grows a little smaller inside.
One morning my mother, weeping,
may find he's flickered out at last,
a small gray heap in an ashtray.
I'll visit, leave the jokes behind,
bring instead a perfect crayoned picture
to wrap around his coffin.

When Our Mothers Die

We plant gardens.
Tomatoes everywhere, and squash,
and on the edges zinnias
with tiny cups of beer.
Also strawberries, two kinds
of mint, even sometimes
new bushes of white roses.

We accept her rings
and wear them on our hands.
The onyx in gold for everyday.
The diamond in platinum
for evenings, holidays, special
mornings of April sun.
Sometimes we wear her wedding band
on a chain around our neck.

We cook food.
Pasta in heaping painted bowls,
chicken with garlic, rosemary.
We invite many friends
and eat and eat, wine
splashing in crystal.
They admire our flowers, our fingers.
Laughing, we offer sweet espresso
in her perfect china cups.

From

THE KITCHEN OF YOUR DREAMS

(Thorntree Press, 1992)

Adultery

Isn't that the essence: room
to breathe, as in
taking a deep breath
before the plunge, as in
breathe in, breathe out, feel
the tension easing from you.
In certain villages in southern
France the sun fills air
with bay and lavender.
Breathe, breathe: love
waits at the café where chairs
make circles, metal tables
carry the clang of coins.
How many breaths does it take
to walk the curving road
from Calviac? *Breathless*
with anticipation, some folks
simper, why that man is like
a breath of fresh air
to a closet stuffed with lies.
And aren't athletes told to have
good breath control? Run,
run past goats with copper bells,
blackberries promising feast. He calls
to you to say his name, one breath
a sigh of promise spurned, another
a gasp towards life.

And Still That Day the Winter Light Held Speech

Anduze, New Year's Day 1988

And still that day the winter light held speech
as dark as water of the mountain stream's
hard coursing past white stone. I felt you reach
your hand for mine, as though to share the dreams
kept distant in night's waking; but again
it fell away, unsure of love's reply.
We glanced at shuttered houses, hatted men
who nodded greeting as we passed them by.
Does heart's first answer always come to this?
A secret question pressing tight the lips
that used to open gladly in a kiss
of vows and laughter? How such silence strips
the soul of morning, as it did that day
when we walked wordless, everything to say.

A Slow Bottle of Wine

he taught me how to drink
a slow bottle of wine
how to make it last
a whole purple afternoon
the fullness lingering
bright and mellow on the tongue

France in August is a field
of lavender gone crazy blue
in need of harvest but not
ready for the sharpened blade
to cut the source of blossom
Oh how the music calls

bamboo forest makes a cool tall
place where stories happen
in the garden of the lotus
a green pool awaits
wishes from new lips
that promise love   *love*

midnight in Monoblet: sound
of paper streamers tearing
C'est la fete! C'est la fete!
all of summer seeming
one long walk to a parked car
black laughing eyes demanding

golden ring   legal promise of forever
tossed into a fountain of hard dream:
marriage fades to fog in this
new landscape of long sun
white rocks along cool riverbank
all the boundaries a heart wants

goats clanking copper bells   the Monday
market with bright earrings in the shape
of ripened grapes   pale castle gleaming
on the mountain in our view
from shuttered windows: how to know
what moments will determine who we are?

I had his baby and the months
of not forgetting southern sun
adultery a promise far beyond
mind's comprehension *oh the fountain*
with the face of Pan pretending
all is now and ever can be frantic dance

a slow bottle of wine I tell you
seems the life and is the life
in love where a woman wanders
full of wanting   free of time
all her years the taste of summer
rising with his name

The Kitchen of Your Dreams

On the wooden counter rests a bowl
heaped with oranges you didn't pick
that Christmas Day in Cagliari

when you knew you'd bear his child.
By the door a cat comes crying,
face round as a full sea moon

above the beach where lovers lean
into each other against the wind.
A radio by the sink plays a song

in a language you will never speak
except for one word, *basta,*
enough that word, *basta.*

Are you making a cake of seven
layers, cheese and chocolate heavy
and dark for midnight's sweet repast

with fireworks loud in the streets?
Oh, drink the old wine, feel
its crimson fingers take you

dancing past Phoenician faces
on the hill above the harbor.
Here you have complete command

of memory: reshape it; make his fist
a rose, his curses lasting compliments
for the banquet of your heart.

Watching Her Sleep

This long past midnight, darkness
is a way of life forever
circling outward, hungry spiral

where the hours meet the stars.
After milk, after arms' embrace
within our mirrored blue-eyed

gaze, my newborn daughter
lies beside me on my single
bed where I sit watching

the flicker of her dreams.
This tiny form, this curl
of fist and curve of mouth,

once grew inside me, part
of every breath and step
until she moved in her own

oneness, daring to be born,
all cream and roses and full
joyful noise against the silence

my own life had become.
Watching her sleep, I know
a fierceness where my heart

once beat alone and didn't
comprehend its loneliness, half-
stanza of a poem that thinks

itself complete. In this new
reach of night where appetite
becomes a future, I find

stillness makes warm certainty
of time, each moment
a calm rhythm more

illuminating to my *why*
than any reeling sunstruck day
of inward rushing light.

I Wear My Stretch Marks Like Tattoos

to show
I am a woman
whose belly has billowed
a mainsail on a pirate ship
on its way to treasure
a queen-size-bed top sheet
on a new clothesline in March

they make silver parentheses
around my freckled navel
tiny river tributaries
from the cold spring of my joy
pattern rising to the touch
like fired-rice-grain china

and oh
the way the sunlight catches
above my satin hipline skirts
when the music births itself again
and I start moving I start
moving and with my daughter
dance

From
SKYROS

(Foothills Publishing, 2001)

Stones

for Suzanne

The pink ones draw us first, that rose of dawn
from sleepless nights of love remembered, full
and perfect as smooth Aphrodite's shell
and just as sea-swept as two hearts alone.
The green ones next, deep dark cat's eye at noon
or ancient pines left standing safe and tall
with roots stretched deep into a rainless hill
above the remnants of an ocean shrine.
Our bodies bend with fingers reaching out
to touch the curves of color, wrest them free
from wave-tossed sand into our hands where hot
and dry transform their brilliance to pale gray.
More softly now they offer inner gleam,
a weighted wisdom, talisman of dream.

Painting on the Beach

for Piers

A naked father and a naked son
move slowly where soft waves pull summer's gold
to green and blue above bright pebbles rolled
around their feet. As they walk on as one,
a body formed and forming, lit by sun,
instinctively we sense a myth so old
our fingers rise in a new way to hold
smooth brush and pigment for what must be done:
the re-creation of a world we need
as much as food and dream, as only art
will give us wholly if our minds can heed
what calls to us from deepest pulse of heart.
The man speaks words and takes the young boy's hand;
we reach for colors—ours—of sea and sand.

Song

for Trixi

Beneath a round moon, red as summer's heart,
they gather in a circle on the sand,
her hand a wand inspiring with art
the deepest reach of music where they stand.
Waves flow; dark pebbles shine in glimmered white
as phrase by phrase her lyrics rise in air
and give a fuller body to the night
already rich and wide with answered prayer.
She's come to this old shoreline from a place
hard-swept with shadow, cold as lightless eyes—
thin years the steady beauty of her face,
kept soft with laughter, modestly belies.
She shapes in words the courage she has found,
transforming them with breath to purest sound.

Frayed Hem

In white and black he sits down in the bar,
makes gesture with two fingers for a drink
yet sits there quite alone, his dark gaze far
away as though he's come here just to think.
A cigarette burns gray where his curved hand
extends from rolled-back sleeve, his elbow bent
and leaning on a knee cocked steady and
assured (it seems) as though unplanned, unmeant.
Alone, in search, so many people try
to offer this same face, a distant stare,
a lack of smile as though they must deny
the need for touch from someone who will dare.
He finishes his drink, gets up to leave,
his shoes too smooth, loose threads upon his sleeve.

Carrying the Prayer

for Sharon and Antonio

I reach out, touch the oldest wall of stone
I can imagine touching, one by one
my fingers each a song of praise alone
near hilltop where the goat-clad ones still run
bell-hung with heavy music. Here I find
a layered temple, Pan to Christ, and more:
Athena moves to Mary in these lined
and sculpted marble fragments on the floor,
the faded words on windows' arch, the groove
for candles' flame—yet brilliant sky takes hold
through crumbling curving roof as though to move
beyond grand Byzantine of painted gold.
Once frescoes graced this chapel, bold and bright;
now lizards turn and dance within new light.

Katarina's Cats

They gather carefully, green eyes aware
of sudden movement, tattered ears alert
for voice and step of someone who'll take care
instead of dealing out another hurt.
In Greece it's chance if animals are loved;
more likely they'll be tolerated, seen
as luxury or nuisance to be shoved
aside and shunned as useless pests, unclean.
Some people let them come into their home
or set out dishes filled with table scraps,
but seldom are they taken into laps
or freed of fleas that plague them as they roam.
The island has no vet; when kittens come,
kind Katarina kills them, all but one.

Rupert Brooke's Grave

Black goats surround the site where he now lies
in monument of words on polished stone
beneath slim olive trees where few bird cries
disturb the desert silence. Here alone
his mortal self was buried, dead at sea
and brought to this small isle he'd just begun
to love as soul's clear haven, poetry
a bold blue breezeswept sky of hot gold sun.
We've come here quietly today to share
a poem in thankful tribute, and to walk
where he last walked on land, the arid air
reminder of our frailty as we talk.
My daughter finds a stick and stirs dried leaves,
unearths a horned white skull where spider weaves.

Finding the Way

for Dina and Yannis

You have to feel the stones beneath your feet,
their polished weight, their heft of history,
each slope and curve of ancient narrow street
a new direction you learn gradually.
Walk cautiously—strong supple shoes are best—
until your bend of arch and push of toe
develop a sure dance of reach and rest
along the routes you slowly come to know.
This village calls out names some recognize—
your own, if you are lucky—hidden ones
that twist and turn with truth past compromise
and chart a map of stars from separate suns.
To walk the streets of Skyros is to learn
heart's most important word for home: *return.*

From

DREAMING HOW THE HOUSE OF LOVE BEGINS

(Pudding House Publications, 2002)

The Beets Poem

Beets: now there's a subject.
Dark red, rounded, hard as—
well, hard as beets.

I know a woman
who grew a garden last summer,
planted it with nothing
but lettuce and beets.
The lettuce didn't grow
but she had plenty of slugs
and beets, plenty of beets.
Now whenever anyone visits her
she takes them down cellar,
says, "See my beets?"
And there they are, pickled,
row after row of dark red jars
no one will ever open.

Someone else I know
always asks for beets, no matter
what kind of restaurant we're in.
Even at the beach
he'll go up to the hot dog stand.
"Got any beets?" he'll say.
And when the man at the grill
just stares at him, he sighs
and turns away, and spends
half an hour just gazing at the waves.

I know what you're thinking.
Why don't I introduce these friends,
have them both to dinner
one night, serve vegetarian?
It's not so easy.
Remember, beets is our subject,
and beets is what I hate about them both.

How To Eat in the House of Death

Bring a pie made of roses, crust cut
out in tiny hearts to let the heat
escape. Use a strong plate
stained by decades of baking
by a mother who smoked too much.

At all costs, come alone. If
you ask a lover to join you
your lips will not touch again.

Walk through the door smiling; greet
your host with the silver toupee. His
wife will graciously take your coat,
lead you to the wine. Pour first
from the bottle with a thin green neck,
tip your glass to the light, then
reach for the crystal decanter brimming
with the wings of a thousand bees.

On no condition, raise a toast. If
you utter a syllable of thanks,
you will swallow your tongue forever.

Join the others. Men with moustaches,
women in tweed and satin suits,
tasteful frills in their hair. When
you are introduced to him, welcome
the guest of honor to your city
and notice his bedroom eyes.

Without fail, make no jokes. If
you try to charm anyone with laughter
your mouth will disappear.

Approach the table spread with platters
and bowls. Lilies light it, fragrant candles.
Spoon some of everything onto your plate,
exclaiming compliments. Demand to know
who made the potted pig's breath, the bread
in the shape of revenge. Give modestly

the list of spices you mixed. Sit
and talk and eat and eat
until one more swallow will kill you.

Absolutely, ignore the faces peering
in through darkened windows. If—
well, no need to warn you.
They are hungry too.

Dreaming How the House of Love Begins

1.

In a room with white walls waits a paint bucket, new, only a few streaks of white dripping down the sides. I walk through the doorway in blue denim pants, no shirt on, no shoes, a single snake bracelet on one upper arm, the other arm carrying a big green book full of many words and pictures but no sentences, no paragraphs. When I reach the center of the room, I turn slowly in a circle and seven windows change to red hibiscus blossoms, promising me something, promising me I will never be lonely again.

2.

I open the letter and it tells me she is dead. Crayfish stew is cooking on the stove and the spice rack is half-empty. With one hand I pick up a bag of marbles clear and beautiful as blackberry brandy. One by one I drop them onto the floor someone has just painted white, white.

3.

The cat curls up on a couch I have never seen before. He is small. Bright-eyed, with a tail orange as lifesavers. *Some Cheshire smile* I think and then turn away before he can disappear. A woman wielding a small black brush enters the room half-naked. She is trying to tell me she has to work here, that soon the paint will dry to dust if I don't go away. I stare at her as if she is a stranger plucking flowers from the center of my eye.

Someone Warm, You Know Him

a friend of mine
a very gentle man
with laughing light blue eyes

we're at a bar
and he starts talking
tells me about Vietnam
how he enlisted
so he wouldn't have to go there
went anyway
and became a star
the man who could shoot dimes
high in the air
automatically without thinking
the man who would shoot anything moving
clay   bushes   men
children

his eyes are laughing again
as he tells me
it took him six years
to break the reflex

now he can sometimes miss
when something moves in the woods

Sand

My father knew the jungle, though
he never talked about what happened
there exactly, only some
sharp nights I remember when
he'd cry to Mom, to me. "It never
stopped," he'd say. "The rain. We couldn't
get dry, the beds, the bandages
damp, no way to stop it." He wouldn't
ever speak about the wounds, the pleas,
the faces closed away toward death
when what he could do was done.
"Thank God you're a girl," he'd say
and touch my face, my hair. "You won't
ever have to go, they'll never
make you go." And Mom would nod.

But here I am, the age he was.
I try to send them letters: what
to say? The air sucking even
at the ink inside my pen, it seems,
the light a thirsty mouth. *Another doctor*
in the family—they both were proud
but I still see my father's face
when talk of troops began. "You shouldn't
have to go"—his voice a whisper forced
from all the stories he'd locked in—
"Let someone else. Not you." I know
he lives again with me the months
of body after body. I understand
his need to speak of rain. "The desert's
everywhere," I write. "The wind. It never ends."

My Daughter, Ten, Dresses as an Alien

This Halloween she doesn't want to see herself
in Princess pink and gold, in Emerald Lady gleam
of Oz, even last year's sparkled onyx satin
Woman Who Came From the Night Storm Sky.
No—"nothing pretty this time," she says, and so
we search for weeks for just the right mask,
a dream of bulging opalescence, huge eyes
that make the planets small, the world a frail
glass marble. Black pants, black silvered jacket,
sleek black shoes set to step through space,
and from her neck a braided ribbon of light
holding a single perfect circle she'll use
to draw others to her power. Dusk comes,
the pumpkins we've cut into demons and cats
glowing against time's grin. Before candy,
before the doors that will open and close,
I photograph her where she once stood pretty,
this daughter, my creature, her strange new face
turned upward towards the reachable moon.

Old Women Crying on the Beach

Alone, I hear them.
Walking here where waves
make tiny white-maned stallions
in the dark. Their voices carry
cadences of story I can't
comprehend but deeply feel
in the place where reason ends.

Whale song others say. *The moan*
of rigging in high wind.
The inside of your own
long yearning. And they laugh.

Walking here I almost see
the women let their hair down
in the dark to trail along
the stallions' flanks, still murmuring,
still moving me to join them
beyond tears. Who dares to say
to me they are not real?

They ride the dark. The hands
they lift from flying manes
are tipped with stars and stars.

Prey

The wolf of love
is a precious monster
that howls at winter's
thinnest edge. Eyes

like a piece of moon
gone searching, tongue
a hidden flame of night,
he prowls the blue

place we need most,
growls ice into our dreams.
Feed him peacocks
with amethyst beaks, buy

him a collar of stars:
he'll drink two golden cups
to your health, laugh
angels into sharp dust.

Ithaca

Today at the Farmers Market
goat cheese, tiny tart grapes,
a catnip toy, one loaf of George's
whole wheat bread, two baskets
of Red Havens picked this morning
seven miles away. The good life:

that's what we say, all those
who work for not enough money
in order to stay in this town
where bookstores beckon on a dozen streets
and three hills curve up green and steep
above the swan-necked lake.

The Iroquois Nation knew this land
as holy spirit place, told stories
that have sunk into the weeds.
Now we who call it our home
summon spirits with different names:
ease, struggle, love. Living

here along the edges of gorges
we give our reasons, smile,
minds knowing only half of why
our breath needs this gray sky.

Dream: The Visit

for Lorraine

I have come to a house
of sudden beauty: blue rooms,
lamps of crystal, bowls
of dahlias gathered from the lawn.
All is made of colors
like sunlight through glass.

A tall woman walks here.
She has made this place.
Her eyes express a willingness
to talk with me. She offers
plums in a sturdy basket.
I reach for one, and bite.

Hours later she says to me,
"Write this, all this, in a poem."
I tell her such a task
may take me all my life.
She smiles. The plum tree
is made of afternoon.

From
WISE WOMAN

(Anabiosis Press, 2003)

Wise Woman's Friend Gets Interviewed
About How the Power Begins

for Rose

sure she's a little
different always was
the smallest kid in her class

looks into things
the way a needle slides
clean through scarlet silk

climbed a roof once
where the stars shot gold
into her sixteen years

I've heard her sing
on a stage with no one
able to reach her voice

she's pepper on bread
she's rain in December
she's hair that curls beyond curl

catch her dancing
some silent Sunday:
she'll spin your blood to joy

Wise Woman Explains to God
Why He's Sometimes in Her Dreams

I've always had a vague appearance,
disappearing into poems
like sea gulls after the last good bite,
like violets, like a stone.

I look into a mirror
and find syllables, breath
caught between a sun-hung dawn
and dolphins circling back for song.

My name? Silver sand between
fingers in love with birth.
I'm a swamp, a camel,
a woman refusing

to let her leg be a lamp.
And you? Come spell with me
the words to leave a dark tongue
tingling: *enough* we'll say *enough*.

I've always found myself
more quickly in another's eye,
appetite for moment's beauty
a rat's star, burning, red.

Wise Woman Talks About Her Sister,
the One Most People Shun

When Death comes riding on her crimson broom,
heed her. Sing praises to her copper eye
that counts silk threads before they reach the loom
and spiders them to patterns a dark sky
calls friend. Her voice will moan your name again,
again dance splendid in her wild silk dress
to all the music she can make as men
and women whirl between heart's no and yes.
Her smile? A snake's revenge. Her hands? Two thorns
torn swiftly from a wilting rose. Her flight
has magicked her between the curving horns
of moon that offer respite from deep night.
Embrace her; kiss the place her teeth and tongue
swear love, where you will be forever young.

Wise Woman's Friend Reveals Why
She Has to Keep on Dancing

I had a daughter once.
Surely I had a daughter?
But she disappeared into a horizon
my fingers could not reach.
Maybe it was with a man
who rode a wild-eyed horse,
sweating black flanks between her thighs
and her smile a crimson slash.
Maybe it was towards a city

with lights higher than any hearth
can offer a sane safe world.
I still have a photograph:
her perfect smooth blue hat,
her hands around small roses.
Was that a person
who swelled my body,
pushed hard into light
as I screamed? I dream

now of brass unicorns, her
stroking and grasping their polished
full horns, a country—France?—
calling out her name,
the name—did I give it?—she
scorns as obscene, the world
unsane, unsafe, untouched
by an aging woman unable to be
the mother a wild girl needs.

From

KATHARYN HOWD MACHAN: GREATEST HITS

(Pudding House Publications, 2004)

Hazel Tells LaVerne

last night
im cleanin out my
howard johnsons ladies room
when all of a sudden
up pops this frog
musta come from the sewer
swimmin aroun an tryin ta
climb up the sida the bowl
so i goes ta flushm down
but sohelpmegod he starts talkin
bout a golden ball
an how i can be a princess
me a princess
well my mouth drops
all the way to the floor
an he says
kiss me just kiss me
once on the nose
well i screams
ya little green pervert
an i hitsm with my mop
an has ta flush
the toilet down three times
me
a princess

At the Veterans Hospital

In Aphrodite's deep and fullest hue
I dance again the halls of Ares' breath
and touch the shadows, celebrating *who*
instead of *what* within these walls of death.
My ankles offer golden bells that sing
of light and wonder, as my hands reach out
rich rhythm-echo of bright zills that ring
the names of Love, close whisper to far shout.
How is it War can use a man like stone
to crush another, smiling proud and bold,
then drop him cracked and breaking, left alone
to crumble into dust as he grows old?
Again I whirl, my hot pink veil held high
to every trembling smile, each waking eye.

Leda's Sister and the Geese

All the boys always wanted her, so
it was no surprise about the swan-
man, god, whatever he was. That day

I was stuck at home, as usual, while
she got to moon around the lake
supposedly picking lilies for dye. Think *I*

would have let some pair of wings catch me,
bury me under the weight of the sky?
She came home whimpering, whined out

the whole story, said she was "sore afraid"
she'd got pregnant. Hunh. "Sore"
I'll bet, the size she described, and

pregnant figures: no guess who'll get
to help her with the kid or, Hera forbid,
more than one (twins run in our damned

family). "Never you mind, dear," Mother said.
"Your sister will take on your chores."
Sure. As though I wasn't already doing

twice as many of my own. So now
I clean, I spin, I weave, I bake,
fling crusts to feed these birds I wish

to Hades every day; while she sits smug
in a wicker chair, and eats sweetmeats,
and combs and combs that ratty golden hair.

Les Salles-du-Gardon

And what if you hadn't hit me.
Hadn't swung your arm backhanded
against the curve of my eyes and mouth,
your blind father right across the table
confused: what did I murmur wrong?

And again, later, back in Marseilles,
after my broken French had explained
you could never, never do it again,
simple candles and the harbor lamplight,
wine in strong clear glasses—then

your rage uncoiling like a creosote rope
within the storm of midnight. What
if you hadn't opened that drawer
and pulled the gun from its careless corner,
in your other hand the unsheathed blade—

you sneered you could easily kill me,
but I wasn't worth it, a woman.
Two weeks pregnant with my daughter of roses,
the child you'll never know we made
because I fled through winter rain

back to America, to silence.
What if you'd hidden the fist
of your laughter till later, longer
in love's warm rooms, and I
had stayed behind time's doors

and learned to believe you were God.

Potatoes

for Eric

It's the way he slices
clean potatoes, boiled just
soft enough to fry in oil
with salt and onions:
she's known a dozen men
who can't compare. They might
add pepper, garlic, even
splashes of paprika red
as midnight lace; but none
have had his fine musician's
hands, the flick of wrist
that works the spatula
in perfect time, preventing burn.
He knows the kitchen
of her dreams, all right,
and fills it up
with simple spices he's aware
will flower in her mouth.
When he carries her
the polished platter, heaped
with feast for eye and tongue,
how she sings in praise of fragrant
food as good as winter sleep,
his love waiting at the table
for her to raise the fork and eat.

From

SLEEPING WITH THE DEAD

(Finishing Line Press, 2004)

Drift

for George Drew

We do not eat swans,
those curves of almost-silver
movement, white as dream cloud,
pure against the blue and gray
of river, pond, lake, our eyes.
We know they cannot walk

with grace on land, but only in
the liquid air beyond our reach,
rich realm of fairy tale. Swans
figure in our deepest sense
of self, in stillness, flight;
brother princes' feathered prison,

ugly duckling's rippled mirror,
Leda's golden thrust toward war
beyond the storm wings' rape.
We dare to touch them, seldom
holding on for long, sudden knowledge
of hiss and heft a new beginning

to shape the face of our fears.
In 1984 in England's
full calm currents of the Thames
the body of a girl was found
drowned and scarred by beaks'
fierce bite, song a silent swim.

The Poem at the End of the World

The hinges that constrain it
sometimes rust, or bend,
or even snap off when the sea
turns wild, emeralds angry as eyes.

A snake curves around it,
complacent, rising up for air
when the phoenix shouts a word or two,
sarcastic in wild flames.

It is made of brothers kissing
wrong, and the sting of coffee
sweet and good, and a dance of hips
that glitter in glass beads.

A woman found it once
when she was seventeen.
She thought it held a dead man,
her dreams still swimming, light.

The Man Who Hated to Watch the Stars

for Steve Moragne

He thought to linger, hoping life might hold
a cataclysmic change, a way new breath
could carry him beyond dull future's *old*
that predefined the pattern of his death.
He worked, drank wine, sat sullen in the sun
regarding others' lack of choice as sure
harsh evidence he was the only one
who understood the universe as pure
tormentor. Only one? And what of she
who lingered on the sidewalk, breaking stride
to raise her eyes to gabled roof where he
dramatically set scene for suicide?
She watched him fall, the black edge far above
a brave new world, her sudden word for *love.*

Sleeping with the Dead

They come into our dreams
as though they have the right to move
again the arms we know are ash
buried, scattered, kept
in polished urns on old pianos
draped with tapestry fringe.
They laugh at us, or say
You never knew my eyes were blue,
or smooth our hair with ivory combs
plucked from fairy tales.
We turn, and mutter, and turn
again, trying not to see
the way their faces catch the sun
and offer us thin rainbows.
So sure they are of our heart's welcome,
so sure they are we live for them,
they light their pipes, kick off tight shoes,
ask for coffee—sugar, no cream—
and never let on they've forgotten our names
as they sip and sip at fragrant steam.

Dear Blue:

Thank you for allowing
me my fists.
Thank you for your face
of good brown eyes
as I circled my feet
around your sitting body.
Thank you for having
short hair of gray and silver
and a simple golden chain
I could imagine being
salvaged from a sunken ship
swept near a living reef.
Thank you for not
speaking as I bent my head
against your covered knee,
as the turquoise beads around my ankle
rippled their tiny bells.
You are a stranger
and cannot know
my brother has just died.
His eyes were the palest color
when he chose suicide.

                    Sincerely,
                    The Woman with a Necklace of Glass

From

REDWING: VOICES FROM 1888

(FootHills Publishing, 2005)

Tess Clarion

I might have found a house, a home,
even a barn or weathered shed
with open door to welcome me
in full-cut frock, my belly huge
and ready. Too many miles alone—
what choice had I?—the horse fatigued,
the flivver jolting this way, that,

and suddenly a tiny inner
kick that loosed birth's waters warm
and certain. She was my second; I knew
the clench and pull. No time to hunt
for bed or rush-strewn floor: I clambered
down to roadside pasture, hoping
for a level place of moss and grass,

my petticoats for rags. How long
I pushed—the swells of breathlessness
and breath—who knows? A cloud-whorled sky
and patient grazing horse in harness
the only witnesses to blood
and cord and sharp beginning cry
as tiny dark-haired daughter met

the light and rose to breast in my
glad hands. We lay in summer's lap
adrowse, sun shifting gloom to gleam,
sweet clover at my elbow, pain
a shared commitment, bodies' bond.
I think a redwing called, I think
the nearby stream sang both our names—

but memory's a trickster when
a woman's merged with God and given
love the shape of life. I knew
my husband still awaited me
the next town over, anxious for
my help, his hip so badly bruised
he could not walk nor ride; but I

let time take her and me along
in goldswept journey lying there,
breeze like softest feathers astir,
our foreheads' sweat a halo. *Angel*
I mused, her mouth my mouth, her hands
such small curved stars. *We'll always share
deep summer's voice, and wings to soar*

through air.

Janet Dobb

Heat's set in early. June, already
chicory in bloom, that blue no eye
could ever be, and lilies orange
as a fencepost tomcat daring the sun

to answer back his yowl. Peonies
went through in a finger's snap, roses
swelled so fast a woman could walk
and smell her wedding day again

on every grassy path. *Too much, too soon*
I say. *Good strawberries need time.*
But you just laugh at me again,
and say *Go stain your hands,* and touch

my back where my back makes wings, kiss
me on the sly. Tomorrow we'll sugar
and soak and stir, wooden spoons
in big black pots, the kitchen a world

of hell and heaven so sweet the air
is all our mouths will need. Clear glass,
clean wax, the wide-planked table waiting
to hold the jars of cooling jam....

Two women working, windows wide,
sweat on our lips, eyes sharing stories,
neighbors together in strawberry time,
summer ripe as our love.

Emely Dunton

I hear his horses clop on cobblestone,
their harnesses' brief music all that breaks
the silence of my days. In here alone
I know a special kind of time; it takes
my breath and makes new stories no black book
has ever held. "And how are you today?"
he asks, his crow's face taking on a look
my heart screams out *Trust not!* I've learned to say,
"Much better, Doctor, thank you, very calm"
—while sharp within me my rage grows, a knife
I'd use to cut away these walls no balm
of medicine can make me call good life.
Look at him now; I see it in his eyes:
he fears and hates what waits beneath my lies.

Jane Anne Dunton

They took Emely away last week.
They said she needed rest, could not
take care of herself as she should.
"A grown woman shouldn't act like that,"
they said, "getting so frightened and sad."

Yes, there were days on end she didn't
smile, wouldn't change her collar, hardly
touched the food on her plate.
But she'd speak to me: "Dear sister, don't
despair. There's more stars in the sky than you see."

"She's always read too much," said Mother,
"when she should have been making friends and met
young men, the right young men."
Father just stared and shrugged and muttered
a few vague words about weak blood.

It happened fast: the day they found her
burning her hair in a china bowl.
She'd cut it off, first time
in her whole life, and there it lay,
black nest aflame in stinking air.

Now she's gone to someplace quiet,
no books or papers allowed, no scissors
and no pens. "A poem
is like a part of you set free,"
she told me once. Oh, Emely.

Bessie Fenton

They laughed when I said I'd do it, eat
the worms. *Stupid girl, you wouldn't
even touch one. Liar, liar!*

But I showed them. I marched right to
the place where they'd been digging, black
dirt all damp and smelling of spring.

One, two, three—I swallowed,
thinking of little birds in nests,
hungry fish in a blue, blue stream.

The boys went quiet—none of them
could speak—till Billie Gray began
to strut around and sneer at me:

*Worm eater! Worm eater! Bessie is
a worm eater!* Then they all ran off
still whooping like a pack of hounds.

I sat there, knowing only that
I couldn't cry. Now they'll tell
the others, make fun of me in school—

but I don't care. I challenged their
whole world of who is strong. They have
to run and try to change the rules.

Sara Ellen Flood

I'm painting again. I can't help painting
blue and blue and blue beyond
what any mountain has ever offered
whether I dream or am awake
here in this house where all is lovely
well-oiled wood and crocheted cotton
and my younger sister's bright-eyed dog
stares at me for flavored biscuits
he's not supposed to get.

Today I read another story
about a dragon left too long
alone in a cold sharp-cornered cave
with only its own flaming belly
to keep it alive till the hero came
looking for rubies, looking for gold,
looking to kill a long-fanged monster
whose eyes are cracked and raging mirrors
bleeding at the edge.

My family? They know everything
they need to know of who I am:
a quiet girl, my long hair combed
and wrapped with pins around my ears,
fingering buttons, smoothing lace,
slipping away without a word
to where my world is white and wide
and waiting for my hand to share
the colors in my head.

Catherine Gray

When my parents died, we came to live
with Hiram and Huldah Gray. They took
us in, no hesitation, gave
me my own room, blue pansy faces
bright on every wall, kept Billie
in a cradle by their bed. I called
them Aunt and Uncle as the pain
became a faded piece of everyday.

At eight years old how can a child
believe the lesson of death? I thought
that when the spring came maybe Mother
would come back to me, she loved
the flowers so. But no, of course,
full summer came and went and left
me quite alone. And I never said
a word to anyone about my hopes.

I learned my books well, grateful to
the Grays, and even took their name.
When Aunt decided I was grown
enough, she took me on as her
assistant. I'd always helped her gather
herbs she grew, but now she taught me
wilder ones, and mushrooms too,
and ways to use them only she could show.

I know I'll take her place someday.
She says I have the gift, and I
can feel I do. I'm seventeen,
and Redwing suits me fine as home.
Besides, in moonlight some warm nights
out in the garden we two tend
I hear a woman singing low
as though to ask her daughter to stay near.

Laura Pearce

When the Gypsies came, your grandmother
made me promise not to go to the woods
where fires blazed and music played
and dark-eyed women danced in coins.
She said they'd steal a girl like me
with golden hair and flower skin
and make me beg in filthy clothes
and feed me scraps of moldy bread.

But the second night the moon rose yellow
and full, and lilacs filled the air.
I couldn't stay; silently I slipped
through the gate, blue shawl a shield
against my family's eyes. I ran
through the town's spring-heavy streets
to where the Gypsies camped, new green
of trees a canopy of lace.

He saw me first, the fiddler, his bow
poised in firelight, black hair a curve
of crow's wing on his brow. I knew
he knew I'd come to them, to him,
for music, night, the sound and smell
of waking earth, brush of pale moths
at my mouth, cry and ache of strings
stretched taut across old polished wood.

Only fifteen, and such knowledge! Slowly
I let the blue shawl fall, and slowly
I stepped near as he smiled and played
the song I had long felt in dream
and never heard and always known.
Slowly I moved; then the tempo quickened,
my feet flickering shadows on ground
dancing, dancing to the Gypsy's touch.

How long? The May stars whirled a course
of newborn constellations, stories
it's taken me years to recall. And after,

he led me to his mother's tent, and spoke.
She brought a tea of sassafras and mint,
perhaps, some spice I've yet to taste again,
and traced her fingers on my palm
and stroked my hair. Both stroked my hair.

What else? I left behind the shawl,
took home instead a fine-spun scarf
she offered from a chest. Yes—the same
that's always hung above your bed, blue
with that single golden coin sewn in
you used to call your star. Remember,
when they try to tell you Gypsies are
no good. Remember, when you dance.

Maura Pearce

She's told her daughter that old tale again.
How many years must she repeat it, eyes
cast back in time to that small wooded glen
where she and I as girls shared pretty lies
of fairies, witches, wolves, and acted out
the stories we had read in gilded books.
I blame myself; as twin born first, no doubt
I should have reined her heart, her dreamy looks
at life as though it offers perfect love
instead of compromise, instead of loss.
Oh yes, she ran that night, spring stars above
dark lilacs, past the church, its Easter cross.
I followed her: there were no Gypsies there;
she kissed our pastor, moonlight in their hair.

From
FLAGS

(Pudding House Publications, 2007)

"The Man Who Had War"

my small son calls the shell-shocked soldier
in the movie set in 1917. Green mountain, lightning
flaring like artillery shock across young dreams
of life: I tell my son the soldier is in pain;
he cannot understand why sky and God
conspire to blast skin to pieces, spill blood
into the heart of earth his mother's bade
him praise. My son: at nine he still accepts
my word, says guns are bad and war is worse,
yet in the toy stores of the wider world
dolls dressed in uniforms hold sway,
rifles pointing brown and hard and clean,
making clear that history says "bear
the arms that shape you into a man"
beyond what any mother, any woman, can.

Bereaved

Her husband turned to silver, burned away.
For months she couldn't make herself believe.
She'd wander home, drink wine at end of day,
stare into dark as though her eyes could weave
a shroud that she could pull apart by dawn
to bring him back, lone hero, from the cave
where shadows rule. Sometimes she'd walk the lawn
beside his garden rows, where he once gave
her tongue a first tomato, perfect, red
beyond all fire's crimson, that hot night
so many years ago. And what he said?
Our love will last as long as there is light....
She's learned to hate the mornings, flow and ebb
of time a dull bedraggled spider's web.

Negative

The day the war ended
she found a photograph of him:
blue shirt, denim jeans,
half-grin on his face.
He'd been the first to kiss
her breasts, his bearded mouth
warm and soft as fire
ran through her from his tongue.
He'd given her a necklace
with a single golden charm:
a bird in flight, soaring
as near as it could to the sun.
Remember Icarus he'd
whispered. *As I fly*
I'll call your name.

She'd just left high school, worked
in the cafe where he'd come in
for breakfast, regular, black
coffee right away. He'd asked
her out and she'd thought *Heck*
why not, two months before college.
Summer's too long to be lonely.
She hadn't known he'd turn
her days to glass, nights
to jasmine in her hair,
soft rain falling.
His voice became the sound
of her own blood singing
praises to the way she moved
beneath him in his bed.

When they parted she wrote him
letters from the dorm:
new people, new books, candles
through the night. She even
tried a poem when the news
broke through—"friendly fire,

troops on the move"—about
great wings in a dark blue sky
and the moon silently watching.
She mailed it, even though
by then he'd come to seem
a shadow of the self she'd been.
*Did he think of me the night
he died?* she couldn't help
but wonder, then set him aside.

Winter

I can't even imagine where you
are as this thick April snow
cancels ballgames, drags down planes,
fills the chapel pond with white and
white that sinks beneath smooth water's

fragile skin. I can't begin
to think of you as anywhere
except the farm, the long fields turned,
apples curled inside curved branches
waiting for hunger's sun. For one

clear moment I can travel back
to hot sweet barn, black raspberries
tumbling heavy in noon sun,
dusk a triumph of fireflies
along the dark slow road (*I told*

you nothing, uttered nothing, brought
books and wine and furniture,
then drove away, always away)
before summer turned to goldenrod
and first frost touched worn eaves, and you

moved your days without a thought
that I might wonder how the trees
will gather light without you there,
blossoms fisted against dark leaves,
ice a weight on time, on prayer.

From

THE PROFESSOR POEMS

(Main Street Rag Publishing Company, 2008)

The Professor First Comes to Grips with Spring

He starts to haunt the streets where she moves slow
and easy down the rows of daffodil.
Her hair blows soft, and he begins to know
a hunger far beyond his strength of will.
She writes him poems sore-tried by student pen
in bland assignment, but they pierce his heart
as though she were a master of deep Zen
blessing him with the wisdom of her art.
"You write so tellingly," he scrawls in red.
"Such sensitivity in youth is rare"—
all while he can't help picturing a bed
with her stretched out upon it, bold and bare.
Semester's end is coming; can he wait?
Yes: A+ first, then—paradise!—first date.

The Professor Reads as a Warm-up Act

(his voice first soft, then moderately loud)
for the More Famous Poet, gray chairs packed
and clanking on worn floorboard. In the crowd
(a generous word) his students show their tact
in hopes he'll see them there and raise their grade.
He offers a new poem about snow
and hears it fall and drift, then seem to fade
to silence where the winds of boredom blow.
But what's this now? A stir of genuine
attention in the slant-back rows designed
to strain the strongest back? Perhaps a line
or two have sparked the audience's mind?
He looks up, gratified, aglow for more—
and sees the wine and cheese come through the door.

The Professor Visits the South of France

He thought perhaps in Arles he might find
the sweet release nightmares had made him seek.
Why not? Van Gogh had tried it, tortured mind
approaching peace in timeless light. A week
or two of vineyards, golden flowers full
of summer's weight? Why not for him respite
from heart's deep reach to her, the awful pull
when longing calls her name? Hell, he knows it
absurd to give her power over him—
a girl, by God, a student who had dared
to reach beyond the page, her hand a slim
deceptive invitation—but he'd cared,
he'd cared! As what man wouldn't? Now he's here—
and finds a sun-dark ghost with but one ear.

The Professor Is Paid to Read His Poems

After the punch supposed to come from green
Hawaiian Isles, the cookies without taste,
the questions about what his couplets mean
and shouldn't poets treat nuclear waste,
he turns at last to see his sponsor smile
and hand him what his soul's endured this for:
the envelope which he must wait a while
to open, nay, must seem now to ignore.
It's common knowledge that a poet's needs
are few—a pen, a glass of wine or two—
and like an air fern his whole being feeds
on atmosphere, beyond what cash can do.
He plays the game of paying pay no mind—
then later finds the check was left unsigned.

The Professor Finds Fire Is the Taste

of dreams gone salt, the deepest brackish stench
a heart can call. One match, a cigarette
let fall—"*Apres moi, le deluge,*" the French
might say and, sneering, laugh—his home a wet
black ruin. Who could think a book could get
so burnt its words would disappear, the drench
of water saving spine and cover, yet
allowing page to turn to ash? The bench
and table where he wrote, the easy chair,
even the drapes he'd let his gaze slide past
to contemplate blue air: all cinder. Where
can he again believe that truth will last?
He wipes his hands—dead smoke has stained them gray—
and looks back once, then slowly walks away.

From
WHEN SHE'S ASKED TO THINK OF COLORS

(Palettes & Quills, 2009)

Virgin Poem

If we lived in the South Sea long ago,
brother, you might have been husband
or lover, taking me in the flowered tent
in ritual, at the festival.
My friends would have brought me shells
and coral, combed my fine brown hair
back from my face, giggling
to think of kisses there. To think
of you, older brother, striding into the tent
to find me there on the sweet soft cloth
stretched upon the sand, my breasts
years from blossom, my hips
straight and narrow as a young palm.
Oh, your manroot there. Your hands
tender and gentle with knowledge
taught you by the village fathers,
tradition, protecting me from evil
spirits that would gather to my hymen.
You would hurt me, yes, but you
would recognize my pain, acknowledge
tears, go on loving me as clean
little sister, and I would know
the pain would end and leave me whole.
How different, brother, in this northern land
where you tore my flesh and left me broken,
dirty secret, shameful sister
knowing eight years into life
love is a jagged island of ice
where flowers never grow.

Swimming with Fish

for Adrienne Rich

Deep, and deeper now, she
undulates into cool silence
redefining green and blue
with silver, shadows, sand.
On the way to sunken treasure,
mesh bag in her moving fist,
she becomes a new bright creature
almost naked, her braided hair
two long thin golden wings.
They come now, the turquoise ones,
eyes like jewels she's searching
for, fins of rippling amethyst,
hundreds of them, helping her,
guides again to the black ship
where she will find new breath
and rise, coins and emeralds
in her grasp, to share, to give
to all the women who cannot
dive as she does, risk her life,
her body's pulse, her eyes.

Foxes

for Sharon Olds

She wrote of foxes, small and densely furred,
dark forests where a girl might go to dream
and name her longings more than what they seem,
a promise shaped by just the perfect word.
Their tails were plumed; the stories that occurred
ran red with motion like an autumn stream
beyond what facts' sharp actions can redeem:
creative lying, deeper than what's heard.
And what of teeth? Hard eyes that shine and stare
with hollowed hunger winter thickens fast?
Small bony paws that reach out sure to dare
the shape of snow's own future, present, past?
She wrote of foxes: it's on us they feed,
the ones who need them, quickened as we read.

The Knife I Gave My Brother

So sharp it could readily
sever a finger to a stump—
as advertised on T.V. stations,
as printed in bold on the box.
In the department store aisle
the huckster drew me in, proclaiming
ease—a bargain—not to be missed—
a special deal on two.
I remember the edge of his eyes

when I asked, "Will you accept personal
checks?" As if I were dirty,
a whore, an affair, he took it
furtively, then shoved the goods
into the innocent bag on my arms.
Long thin cartons, long thin blades,
black handles curved for good grip:
thinking it would count for something,
thinking life might be fair,

I sent one to Connecticut,
another assertion of love.
Months and months went by;
the check was never cashed.
Knife that could cut through anything...
the sturdy hose my brother used
despite my letters, gifts, my calls,
cut perfectly to fit just right
and steal his breath away.

On Halloween I Rearrange My Spice Rack

After all, it's almost baking season:
cinnamon into a new glass jar,
cloves and allspice in small square tins
I take down, polish, set back upon
my woven wicker shelves above
where my striped cats drink water, crunch
dark food from shining silver bowls.
Edge of the year, veil wavering
between human breath and spirit reach

through time no longer time. My mother
waves to me and smiles, her crimson
fingernails around her final cigarette.
My father offers a smooth tomato,
perfect gleaming globe in his curved palm.
My grandmother holds up her wrists
and looks to see if I still wear her
jewelry. Then there's him, my brother,
half-rising from his suicide, mouthing

our pain's secret from far ago, his ashes
thin and trembling with long plea.
All of them call to me through clear air
how they will welcome me, the last.
But my warm kitchen's all around me
and the stove stands bright and clean.
I reach for sugar, deep cups of sugar.
How good the solid wooden spoon
still feels in my old hands!

From

BELLY WORDS: POEMS OF DANCE

(Split Oak Press, 2009)

Mirage

Ten figures swirl across a polished floor
to rhythms beat upon taut goatskin drums
of Araby. Bare heels upraised, steps more
than motion, bellies curved, their glide becomes
a midnight cat, a desert snake, a wave
of wind across oasis pool. Their eyes
compel our gaze—bright fire in dark cave?—
and smooth hips shimmy to the dumbek's rise
and fall, as silken hands reach up and out
to offer music's essence. Who can say
what's real and what's illusion, or who doubt
we do not need to say? True beauty's way
is mystery; our hearts must take the chance
and trust themselves completely to this dance.

With Music Only Women Hear

When Silva dances, snakes
become her hair, her veil,
the sting of tongues against her wrists

glimmering with metal. Moon
begins the slow ride up
to where her naked hands

give thanks, crescent curved
to a scimitar polished
by blue air. A door

swings open into light
and she moves through it, taking
all the ways we see the world

and making them a dream
of eyes. We follow slowly, faces
waiting, wonder mirror bright:

she laughs the kind of laugh
that matters, womb-blood garnet
set in stone, and all the trembling

wands of power set themselves
aflame and burn. Silva
turns and Silva dances

until the oceans roar delight
and we remember why we've come
to join our voices in this night.

No, Superman Was Not the Only One

In secret, Lois Lane wore coins and jewels
draped perfectly against the naked skin
she perfumed with wild jasmine, taunting fools
who'd denigrate her dance as snaky sin.
She called for drumbeat, shook the stage apart
with shift and shimmy, crescent arms upraised
to show the world the power of her art
and how on Earth the Goddess should be praised.
In silvered silk, her pinned-up hair set free,
she swayed and spun and seemed almost to fly
above the smoky air, almost to be
a bird, a plane, sublime in midnight sky.
No morning news reported what she did;
even from Clark she kept her cymbals hid.

Aubade

When I heard all the brouhaha
I rushed out into the street, asked
Sophie and Jane next door just what

the ruckus was all about. "Soap,"
they said. Sure enough, the street
was foaming white and high and all

the kids were running beside, screaming
and laughing and pushing each other in.
Pretty, with the sun out that bright

and rainbow bubbles breaking loose.
Somebody must have poured a box
or bottle by the hydrant—but so

much water? Like a parade it came,
sparkling and slow and making shapes
a person might believe in. Why,

I tell you, Henry, you've been dead
all seven years now but I would
have sworn I saw you rise

and dance on towards me nodding
like David before the ark. A woman
thinks strange thoughts on April days

with the daffodils for sale. Jane says
this city's getting to her at last
and maybe we all should move. But where

else could I skip down in my apron
and find such a sight like a song
in stone: soap

making dreams of morning
light, and us
all smiling along.

Cane

for Jackie, as we continue

In sparkling velvet, blue a hint throughout,
she takes the stage, her hip a thrust of knife
through bread and bone as drumbeat brings about
rich transformation only fullest life
can make real breath and truest reach. No young
embrace of this long art can give so much,
however dexterous and deft among
applauding crowds; it takes a seasoned touch
to ripple through the air of time and move
an audience to know the why and when
of how they've come to live and deeply love
the yes of saying yes despite again.
She carries us in arc of curving gold
as music celebrates a new word: *old.*

Within the Stormy Sky

to dance before a dragon
is to wear your long skirt torn
is to let your sweet hair red and calm
tangle into fire

such a snaky way of being
such a tongue upon your thighs
such a luscious wicked crimson
daring long desire

wear the pure silk no man gave you
the one your mother left behind
her death a delicate permission
to taste what wings can bring

sing mountain
sing black sky behind you
where morning makes its bed
and smiles

the dragon rises full and ready
to take you on her back and ride
past the white skirts with their narrow
rules that say your love's too wide

From

H

(Gribble Press, 2014)

Night Story

She thinks about swans, the woman reading,
and a tall girl with tangled hair
touching the fur of a silent bear
who will become a prince. Needing

a cup of tea, she rises, moves
to put the kettle on for steeping
good hot black to prevent her sleeping
before the clock strikes twelve. Hooves

of a golden horse keep pace across
her heartbeat as she stirs in milk,
remembering a gown of silk
she wore one summer day. *My loss*

is nothing she repeats and then
she pours away the extra water,
waiting for her only daughter
who, hungry, might come home again.

Eyes Through the World

I took her traveling, my daughter,
but she doesn't need any country now
except the one inside her: walls
that shimmer white on white
and pulse with warm sweet heat.
She once was beautiful, my
traveling daughter, her suitcase sewn
with rainbow patches, her sure hands
on doors and windows, strong feet
on beaches and roads. What turned her
to touch only locks and blinds?
We shared a map, my beloved daughter,
and talked of where new years would
take us, writing stories and poems.
Now she smoothly lies, forgets,
sells off souvenirs to keep
breath going with needles and pills.
The heavy sultan holds her close
in his harem without dance.
She stares at me. I pack my bags.
My love doesn't stand a chance.

H

Beer makes you fat, whiskey burns,
and marijuana stinks and clings,
so when she went she went straight
to the point, the long one, skinny, silver, sharp
and bright as an enchanted prince's fingers
promising a star-swung dance. *Nothing*
makes you feel as good as heroin
she tells her brother and me as we
bring her heart-shaped foil-wrapped chocolate
for Valentine's Day, snow falling fast.
She's twenty-one; the hard law says
I can't just take her in my arms
and lock her in a warm high tower
with no doorway to the street.
She stares at us and lies again:
she didn't steal four hundred dollars,
she doesn't know why a trooper called,
these cold shadows that were once clear eyes
come from sweet late nights of reading
precious fairy tales.

How Not to Write a Poem

Allow a loved one's illness
to get in the way of your pen
or keyboard or stick in the sand
or even the voice that calls in
your dreams bellowing villanelles.
Say it's your daughter. Say she's

twenty-two and addicted to dope
so you can't do a god-blessed
thing because she's a legal adult.
Go to Al-Anon, live the Twelve Steps,
whittle your guilt to a small
tight splinter and flick it into

hot flames. The places where you keep
your stanzas will disappear into dust.
Vaguely you'll remember needing
enjambment, metaphors, rhyme—
but they're all forgotten now.
You just don't have the time.

Stark Awake at 4 a.m.

"Worldwide, the UN estimates there are more than 50 million regular users of heroin, cocaine, and synthetic drugs." —The BBC

she sees the ice on her windowpanes
make silver of the night's fake light
and hears her husband sleeping deep
in dreams of their dying daughter.
How to count a thousand sheep?
How to hum long breathless tunes
muffled in a flannel pillow
on a bed a century old?
Instead she sits up on the edge
and fumbles for her dark brown scuffs
and creaks her way out through the door
to new December silence. A poem
hangs taut and stiff out there
but she does not try to touch it.
Time now only for hot tea
in a cup of china roses.
Motherhood is an open hand
with thin fingers flat and useless.

Snow

falls outside my safe brown home
and I am weeping, I am crying:
this house holds two black-striped cats
but God is a distant palace of whim

allowing my daughter to long for a drug
that turns her into thin gray smoke,
vague lips that lie for survival.
Crystals? They're blowing now

swift and silver and silent as hope
only a mother can ask to find
when the body she's birthed and loves
finds heroin is more important

than giving to the wider world
calling out her name. Snow
beautiful and bright and pure
pours down from a streetlit night

here where I dare write a poem
praying that the girl I bore
is able to look out through a window
and wonder at winter sky.

When I Return to Sardinia

I'll be too old to get pregnant again
by a wild-smiled man who made me laugh
as we climbed the hill above the harbor

where St. Francis offers outstretched arms
and the pale stone face of a Phoenician goddess
waits quietly for time to pass. I'll arrive

in summer, not Christmas Eve with boxes
of chocolates wrapped and ribboned, red
garters thrown from wooden windows, small

firecrackers in cobbled streets all bang
and pop and smoke. Maybe the ghost
of the woman with braids will open her

door, new licorice vendors will nod
as I find again the grand cathedral
confettied with weddings' broken china

white and blue and green. I'll go alone—
or take my daughter with me, if she'll
leave her needles behind. We'll walk

on the sand where I walked with him,
shells still the shape of tiny bottles
liquored with gold, with wave-tossed light.

From

WILD GRAPES: POEMS OF FOX

(Finishing Line Press, 2014)

Fox Likes to Look at the Lake

She goes there often, clear edge mottled
with pebbles, old leaves, string from a long-grown
child's new sailboat that broke away
in high wind. Or from the sudden rising hill
at its southern end she watches water
wide and blue and calm and deep

the way sky can be upside down
if clouds disappear, if storm stays away.
Fox envies all who leap and swim
easily when summer happens or autumn
holds warm heavy gold for bare skin
in liquid light. She stays on shore

dry and clothed in soft smooth color
that lets her think she is the lake
stretching far and long away
to where north tells another story
she will hear, will listen to,
but not just now, no, not today.

Wild Grapes

for Suzanne

Fox sees them on the edges of her dreams
when nights are cool and a harvest moon
sings the names of witches. Then she wakes

to reach for them where vines have climbed
high and twisting up certain trees, old ones
whose branches understand full welcome

yields a richer world. Bunched. Tiny. Each
thick-skinned ball of staining fruit
a sample of sun stretched summer long:

just the right cool of autumn nights
to make their sour sweet. Fox
likes to roll them on her tongue, bite

down when her long jaws are full.
Seeds are big and firm and crunchy;
she savors the sounds they make. Grapes

no one's planted but lingering birds
hold a special kind of music.
Fox hums it softly under the breath

her chewing has turned purple, blue,
a good warm darkness deep spells know
can make its own long lasting light.

Red Diamond

Fox likes to drink that wine.
It's the same color as the edge of her tongue
after she's dined on certain rabbits
bred just for her in that potting shed
with its cunning little green roof.
Fox prefers a thin-stemmed glass
etched with initials half an inch tall;
she found it at the Salvation Army
alone on a metal shelf. Sometimes
she offers wine to friends, but Red Diamond
she keeps for herself. Not all riches
should be shared with the world: this one
Fox drinks to her own health.

Fox Visits the Place Where Witches

"The girls might see a dark figure or a small bird and claim that the spirit was pinching, choking, or sticking them with sharp needles."
—The Salem Witchcraft Hysteria

were hanged and buried, pressed
and buried: I AM INNOCENT
BUT I AM BLAMED: Salem

in warm October wind, head-
stones, gravestones, so many
old names carved. Fox

slowly walks and pauses and walks:
birth dates, death dates, chiseled
words that still echo aching

summer 1692
when this small village let the devil
laugh in lying moonstruck eyes.

Fox Knows Through Her Window

soon the high moon will begin
to show itself, no matter its size:
waxing, waning, still the light
reaches sharply into her eyes
and finds the sister fire there
cool, lucid, tinged with shadow
of ivy, heather, holly. Fox

has finished summer, welcomes autumn
in all its chill and gold and smoke,
days shortening breath by breath
and body reaching for warm quilts,
pots of pasta, bowls of soup, sweet
dark molasses for gingerbread
kissed by witch and whisker. She

knows she's Fox and knows she's sure
of season after glowing season
until the day or night poems end
and she becomes a red-furred ghost
still shifting shape and shaping shifts
among the phases far bright stars
surround with steady silver.

Fox Watches, Refusing to Smile

*"Now the crows drop winter from their wings, invoke the harshest
season with their cry." —Angela Carter in "The Erl-King"*

as she hears sky telling soft earth
to harden, shrink, stifle all pulsing
as he who hides in oldest woods

comes forth to command full praise.
*The rusty fox, its muzzle sharpened
to a point, laid its head upon*

his knee Fox reads, resisting, sensing
*A little of the cold air that blows
over graveyards always goes with him*

like the goblins she has conquered,
the gropers at dusk and dawn. Fox
has had to work hard to survive

so many tricksters, so many fools, knows
There are some eyes can eat you
and *His are quite green, as if from*

too much looking at the woods:
her woods, Fox growls, where she'll
keep her own good company, thank you,

resting her muzzle on a strong warm thigh
and making babies the color of dirt
where roots and seeds wait, thriving.

Full Moon

Fox knows it without looking up.
Hot moon. Blood moon.
If she were a coyote
she'd howl her deep throat raw.
If she were a swamp toad
she'd lift jeweled eyes in love.
Instead she starts to dig and dig
into sweet black forest earth.
Light is round. Her womb's ready.
Two kits will breathe tonight.

Linden Tree

Every three months when the moon's half full
Fox meets him here, the praying soldier,
where clean grass grows tall and lush
and starlings have circled until each has found

its balance on a branch. He never has
to open his eyes; she simply makes her red
way to him and lays her muzzle upon
his knees where they bend to touch

firm earth. No matter the season, sky
open or full, he is there and she is there
until dawn calls small dark wings flying.
Fox knows what it is to be a Crone

a lost young man can welcome: magic
in all that she does not say,
the weight of her head, her amber gaze
what quietly helps him find his way.

Fox Watches the Last White Sail

far out on the deep long lake
from where she sits on a curving shore
cool in September, poised for frost,
first sunmost green leaves turning.
She's happy; she's still alive; she's

loved and listened to, assured she's good
enough to write and dance with others
who enjoy her mind, her belly.
Poems and birdflight, grapes and music,
autumn's balance of dark and light:

Fox gazes out across blue water
that seems to disappear to sky
in a beautiful way, wind's clear high edge
in her breath a calm beginning
of knowing how she'd like to die.

From

DARK MATTERS

(FutureCycle Press, 2017)

Path

"I don't know what I want but I don't want this..."
—Anonymous, in PostSecrets, compiled by Frank Warren
(Regan Books, 2005)

He's the shadow in the leaves.
He carries a bag. It has claws.
All I have is my thin red sweater
and I can't ever pause.

When I was seven a carnival clown
tried to get me up to the stage
to toss my kisses into a hat
that sparkled with black diamonds.
"The little girl in the red sweater!"
he called, and gestured with glimmering gloves.
My mother urged me, but I shrank back,
and another little girl—in blue—got
to see her lips make rainbow candy.

My brother's ghost is a wisp of smoke.
I swam his ashes into the sea,
then changed into warm dry jeans
and my red sweater, tight on me.

When I was sixteen I knew a woman
ninety-two who liked to crochet.
I served her breakfast, cleaned her room,
and listened to her stories of France,
how she went to balls and wore real emeralds
and how glad she was she could remember
all this way across the ocean
with others who were old. She gave me
a red sweater when we said goodbye.

Maybe he's a wolf in a fairy tale.
Maybe he's a doctor who wants me dead.
I can't quite see in my red sweater
no matter how often I turn my head.

At thirty-five I went to Sardinia
and easily touched a goddess's face.
The harbor made me shake in awe.

Right next to magnificent Cagliari
small ancient homes were open, too,
and women somber from head to toe
herded their goats and sheep nearby.
I didn't know that I was pregnant
but I wore a red sweater inside my chest.

He slyly moves when I start walking.
Moonlight's never quite enough.
What time is it? What time, Mr. Fox?
My sweater's ragged at its red cuff.

When Your Daughter-in-Law Hates Magic

Hide your spoons.
Mask your gingerbread

as cumin cookies, lemon loaf,
any scent that will put her off

what you offer to the world.
She must never know

how you saved that baby from the sting
of the tiny Mexican scorpion

or how you died on that cold beach
of the lake that shivered your name.

She's married now, to that warm son
you kept alive on your round breast.

Stay somber, quiet, staunch with grace.
When she turns her gaze away

you know you'll go dancing high
to tango with the moon's sharp curve:

your breath rising full and hard
as the broom your clear prayers ride.

Your Mother

for Carla

I saw Kennedy get shot she says
when you were a baby at home.
I took you to Woodstock she says
and you peed where nude people swam.
And now you stitch wings to old keys
and shape giant birds of paper?
You get paid for making art
about books the whole world reads?
You tell your children you must stay
as far from me as you're able?
In the voice beyond her voice
you hear your young self silent.
In secret words she tries to swear
she never let him touch you.
I was there in Dallas she says.
I wore tie-dye on Yasgur's farm.
How could you ever believe I would let
anyone do you harm?

Helen

They say it was my face. No:
let me tell you about marriage.
Silences and swords, a stone house,
my women whispering around me
dull as bees. For years before he touched
our doorsill, I dreamt his voice;

the silver gifts he brought were tiny
mirrors of the girl I'd held inside
too long. Soon I turned willing hands
to weave for him, each thread a piece
of secret song. The peacock blue, the purple
heart of pansies, red a cry of sun

setting over unclimbed hills. *I asked
to go with him.* I knew he watched
me walk across cool tile, my feet
in sandals I yearned to kick away
so I could run to him unbound
by safe convention. Strange strong guest,

reluctant to offend the man he knew
I didn't love, whose hospitality
was heartless, rote, a hand that drops
coins in a beggar's cup without a glance.
One morning when the sun rose white
and helplessly again I moved to stand

beside him where the swans swim slow,
he took my hand in his and nodded *yes.*
All time burst to blossom and I
knew what it was to be the rose.
Swift ships, sting of salty air, my hair
wrapped around his fingers in the dark:

we could have lived forever in that place
of travel, seabirds wailing overhead,
the men around us eyeing me like some
pure stolen chance—how could they know?—and my
hopes free as any muscled gleaming fish
leaping higher than those blue and bitter waves.

Penelope

after Adrienne Rich

The world remembers me for loving him:
sleeping chaste in Ithaca, my heart firm
as the living tree he carved for our bed.
Good Penelope! Faithful and cunning wife
to fool with woof and warp
the suitors who would claim
all that Odysseus left behind.

But a woman doesn't love a man
gone eighteen years, patience be damned!
I learned to love myself and lived
alone, as some might call it, manless,
supposed to weep and dream of his return.
Return? I knew that someday he might find
his way back home, that I'd be here;

yet in the interim there was no loving him,
for love is deeds, not thoughts and feelings
fluttering through the brain and blood.
What I wove on my loom I wove for me.
I dedicated every story in my threads
to bold Arachne, to all women brave enough
to spin the truth of history. At night

I smiled to hear the green and golden song
of growing skeins as I unraveled
images for the next day's telling.
Alone? When imagination looked toward dawn
as toward a secret tryst? When hands
grew daily stronger and more sure
that what they wove was powerful?

My stories broke the silence of the air
around the house, around the women
who watched them with a serious delight
and turned to one another, their eyes bright
with recognition, daring *yes.*
The suitors grew uneasy, called for wine,
insisted that the women dance for them,

and gradually as with one mind
began to shun the room where I sat weaving.
They sensed the presence there
of some new spirit—a calmness
in my smile, a way I had of gazing
at their leering faces unperturbed—
that disconcerted them, sent them away

muttering that something was amiss.
They couldn't read my loom,
saw nothing there but colors
meeting in confusion, if they looked at all.
So it went on. Years passed. I grew
older with the women, and together
we taught their daughters how to weave.

A hundred eager hands reached for the threads
and they surpassed my art so far
that I sat back in gladness knowing
silence would never still the air again.
It was that gladness, not time,
that drove the suitors wild
to claim me, shouting "Choose! Choose!"

And I would have chosen—to save us—
despite my son—had not Odysseus returned.
When he slipped into the hall in rags
and strung the bow, already I
loved him again, willed his success, welcomed
night embraces in the great carved bed.
So, loving, we continue.

And mornings, loving,
every loom a tree of light,
I weave again with the daughters around me,
fingers sure in time's glad reach,
learning from them now, faithful
to the green and golden stories
that celebrate our love.

An Account of My Disappearances

after Jack Anderson

1.

The day of roses.
The day of withered thorns.
With one small bag of paisley silk
I slipped into my small blue car
and drove, drove to Pennsylvania.
Shirts without buttons.
Quilts.

2.

Music gonged and hammered down the hill.
I stayed where I was.
No one saw me.

3.

The oven burned my cranberry muffins
before the priest could arrive.
I fled. New ice
shattered beneath my feet.

4.

The time of seven months.
The time I counted seagulls
like pennies in a fountain.
My mother had been dead
for many years, but still
I traveled South.

5.

Only my voice
like a nymph in a cave
ashamed of loving
a perfect man.

6.

The first time: to New York City.
With the boy I never saw again.
His name was Paul.

7.

The last one: raccoon tracks
in late Spring snow, daughter
of the one who growled and spit.
I put on my leather fox mask.
A red-winged blackbird called.

Prayer Sequence

Tie the first one to a blue balloon,
but don't let go, don't let it rise.
Like a plastic bag murdering a manatee
it could choke a bird.

Shape the second one after a tornado
has torn up all the thriving oaks
next to the teahouse a woman created.
Her black dog barked, saving her.

The third should be purple as spring dusk
on a road used by soldiers to walk to war.
Their socks have rotted. Their boots stink.
Their guns mean nothing anymore.

Pull the fourth from the mouth of a fish
like a coin spent on a Greek island.
It has touched so many travelers
its date is a poem lost in time.

Five: the last, your salvation. A girl
with a body like a painted drawer
will hand you a bone, a jeweled collar.
Bury one. Burn the other. Sing.

Beneath the Tallest Live Oak

You know you are dead.
You are not dreaming; you are dead.
In a swing as bright as the moon
sits the child who fell through skyscraper glass.
In a whirlwind of ashes and bone
laughs the woman who was your mother.
You're wearing a long pink cotton dress
and a necklace of clear glass fishes.
A lizard dares to climb into your hand.
It pulses, settles, stays.

Heavenly spheres are the thousand cicadas
released from their hard monstrous husks.
You remember you were someone else
with a name, hot love, piles of books.
Here you delight in a simple chair
someone carved from very new wood.
Light lingers, palpable with sea.
Your hair is still silver and white and gray
lifted just a bit by the breeze
that pushes through pale jacaranda.

A shadow of a sharp-leafed frond
wavers beneath a rippling web
wide enough for the eye of God
to rest there, summon, glitter.
You remember a prayer you learned
and you let it shape your lips.
The lizard stirs, rises, moves
to the palm of someone else.
The small child waves to you.
You taste your mother's breath.

Acknowledgments

13th Moon: "Five Poets Travel to and from a Poetry Reading Two Hours Away"

Amazon: "Journey Through the Door into Always-Always Land"

Arizona State Poetry Society 2013 Contest Winners' Anthology: "How Not to Write a Poem"

Artful Dodge: "How to Eat in the House of Death"

Blast Furnace: "H"

Blunderbuss: "Night Story"

Buckle &: "Carrying the Prayer," "Potatoes"

ByLine: "Les Salles-du-Gardon," "Winter"

California Quarterly: "Sara Ellen Flood: Redwing, 1888"

Callapooya Collage: "The Professor First Comes to Grips with Spring," "The Professor Is Paid to Read His Poems," "The Professor Reads as a Warm-up Act," "The Professor Visits the South of France"

Cedar Rock: "Pockets," "Virgin Poem"

Chautauqua: "An Account of My Disappearances"

Comstock Review: "Janet Dobb: Redwing, 1888," "The Knife I Gave My Brother," "Wise Woman Explains to God Why He's Sometimes in Her Dreams"

Crosswinds Poetry Journal: "Beneath the Tallest Live Oak"

Early Ripening: American Women's Poetry Now, ed. Marge Piercy (Pandora Press [London, England] 1987): "Ithaca"

Earth's Daughters: "Wild Grapes"

Ellipsis: "Your Mother"

Freshwater: "Stark Awake at 4 a.m."

The Grapevine: "Mirage"

Hanging Loose: "The Beets Poem"

The Healing Muse: "Snow"

The Hollins Critic: "Leda's Sister and the Geese"

The Illinois Review: "No, Superman Was Not the Only One"

The Ithaca College News: "Black Swans"

Ithaca Times: "In This Hotel Called Home," "The Man Who Hated to Watch the Stars," "Within the Stormy Sky"

Kaleidoscope: "At the Veterans Hospital"

Karamu: "With Music Only Women Hear"

Korone: "Watching Her Sleep," "Wise Woman's Friend Gets Interviewed About How the Power Begins"

Labyris: "When She Was the Good-Time Girl, My Mother"

Louisiana Literature: "Drift," "Fox Visits the Place Where Witches," "Fox Watches the Last White Sail," "Sleeping with the Dead"

Measure: "Maura Pearce: Redwing, 1888"

Metanoia: "When I Return to Sardinia"

Mothering: "I Wear My Stretch Marks Like Tattoos"

Mothers and Daughters: A Poetry Celebration, ed. June Cotner (Harmony Books, 2001): "My Daughter, Ten, Dresses as an Alien"

A Natural History of Raccoons by Dorcas MacClintock (Charles Scribner's Sons, 1981): "When They Lined Up for the Ark"

Negative Capability: "My Brother," "When Our Mothers Die"

Nimrod: "Fox Likes to Look at the Lake," "Full Moon," "Linden Tree," "Red Diamond"

Oxalis: "Aubade"

Passager: "Prayer Sequence," "Wise Woman's Friend Reveals Why She Has to Keep on Dancing"

Phoebe: "Wise Woman Talks About Her Sister, the One Most People Shun"

Poetpourri: "The Poem at the End of the World"

Poetry Center 1987 Anthology: "Laura Pearce: Redwing, 1888"

Poetry Center 1988 Anthology: "Helen"

Poetry Center 1989 Anthology: "The Kitchen of Your Dreams"

Poetry Center 1991 Anthology: "Negative"

Poetry for Peace, ed. P. J. Roberts (SandStar Publications, 2002): "'The Man Who Had War'"

Poetry in Public Places (New York City bus placard series): "Sometimes"

The Poetry Society of America Bulletin: "Penelope"

Rapscallion's Dream: "Hazel Tells LaVerne"

Remembering Faces: An Anthology of Women Celebrating Women, ed. Donna Marbach (Palettes and Quills, 2008): "Swimming with Fish"

Rosebud: "Path"

Runes: "Foxes," "The Professor Finds Fire Is the Taste"

Sinister Wisdom: "Emely Dunton: Redwing, 1888," "Jane Ann Dunton: Redwing, 1888"

Slant: "And Still That Day the Winter Light Held Speech"

Snake Nation Review: "Sand"

South Coast Poetry Journal: "Dreaming How the House of Love Begins"

The Southern California Anthology: "Tess Clarion: Redwing, 1888"

Spillway: "When Your Daughter-in-Law Hates Magic"

Spoon River Poetry Review: "Fox Watches, Refusing to Smile"

Still Going Strong: Memoirs, Stories, and Poems About Great Older Women, ed. Janet Amalia Weinberg (Haworth Press, 2006): "Cane"

String Poet: "Her Father's Ghost"

Telewoman: "Dream: The Visit"

Tiferet: "Fox Knows Through Her Window"

Washout Review: "Someone Warm, You Know Him"

West Branch: "Adultery"

Women Artists Datebook 2001: "Bessie Fenton: Redwing, 1888"

Xanadu: "Eyes Through the World"

Yankee: "Blackberry Man," "Old Women Crying on the Beach," "Prey"

About FutureCycle Press

FutureCycle Press is dedicated to publishing lasting English-language poetry books, chapbooks, and anthologies in both print-on-demand and Kindle ebook formats. Founded in 2007 by independent editor/publishers and partners Diane Kistner and Robert S. King, the press incorporated as a nonprofit in 2012. A number of our editors are distinguished poets and writers in their own right, and we have been actively involved in the small press movement going back to the early seventies.

The FutureCycle Poetry Book Prize and honorarium is awarded annually for the best full-length volume of poetry we publish in a calendar year. Introduced in 2013, our Good Works projects are anthologies devoted to issues of universal significance, with all proceeds donated to a related worthy cause. Our Selected Poems series highlights contemporary poets with a substantial body of work to their credit; with this series we strive to resurrect work that has had limited distribution and is now out of print.

We are dedicated to giving all of the authors we publish the care their work deserves, making our catalog of titles the most diverse and distinguished it can be, and paying forward any earnings to fund more great books.

We've learned a few things about independent publishing over the years. We've also evolved a unique, resilient publishing model that allows us to focus mainly on vetting and preserving for posterity poetry collections of exceptional quality without becoming overwhelmed with bookkeeping and mailing, fundraising activities, or too-taxing editorial and production "bubbles." To learn more about what we are doing, please come see us at www.futurecycle.org.

The FutureCycle Poetry Book Prize

All full-length volumes of poetry published by FutureCycle Press each calendar year are considered for the annual FutureCycle Poetry Book Prize. This allows us to evaluate each submission on its own merits, outside of the context of a contest. Too, the judges see the finished book, which will have benefitted from the beautiful book design and strong editorial gloss we have become famous for.

The book ranked the best in judging is announced as the prize-winner in the subsequent year. There is no fixed monetary award; instead, the winning poet receives an honorarium of 20% of the total net royalties from all poetry books and chapbooks the press sold online in the year the winning book was published. The winner is also accorded the honor of being on the panel of judges for the next year's competition; all judges receive copies of all contending books to keep for their personal libraries.